A Day in the life of

Humphrey

The Downing Street Cat

A Day in the life of

Humphrey

The Downing Street Cat

AS TOLD BY DAVID BRAWN

HarperCollins*Publishers*

First published in 1995 by
HarperCollinsPublishers
77-85 Fulham Palace Road,
Hammersmith, London W6 8JB

Text © David Brawn 1995

David Brawn asserts the moral right
to be identified as the author of this work

For HarperCollins: Bob Warner, Steve West, Ray Barnett, Russell Jones, Graeme Andrew,
Polly Powell, Barbara Dixon, Bridget Scanlon, Vanessa Ratcliffe and Becky Humphreys

The publishers thank the following photographers, individuals and organisations for their
kind permission to reproduce the photographs in this book:
Agencie France Press, Greg Evans International, Hulton Deutsch Collection Limited,
John Muir, John Sturrock/Network, Mark Fiennes, Mirror Syndication International,
"PA" News Photo Library, Peter Jordan/Network Photographers Limited, Ray Barnett,
Rex Features Ltd, *The Times*, Solo Syndication Ltd, The Press Association Ltd,
Topham Picturepoint

A catalogue record for this book
is available from the British Library.

ISBN 0 00 471000 2

Printed and bound in Great Britain
by The Bath Press

Dedication

To all my friends at the Cabinet Office,
for forgiving me for being 'the cat who deserted the
thinking ship' (as well as the various bird incidents)

To the Royal Army Medical College, Millbank,
for taking me in and looking after me in my hour of need
(even if they did think I was a tatty old stray)

To the Blue Cross who (unknowingly) saved one or more
of my nine lives

And to my publishers, Robin and Polly,
for allowing me the chance to put my side of the story
(and who both sound to me like a light snack!)

Introduction

The Downing Street Ears

'Eyes, 2. Nose, 1.' I have been reliably informed that this is a good way to introduce a book of political memoirs. I guess it is meant to be a clarification of one's credentials to do one's job properly. In which case, just to cover all the tools of the trade, 'Ears, 2. Teeth, 30. Tail, 1.' Which says it all really.

I am Downing Street's official mouser. A former stray, I was adopted by the Cabinet Office to rid them of unwanted visitors. Unfortunately, I have only been effective in driving out the rodents so far, though I do have a rather good stare I practise on other undesirables. My real talents are in the extermination of terrorists of the feathered variety, but to my surprise my actions in this area seem to have been less well received by my employers.

I am no stranger to life at the top. In the course of my duty, I rub shoulders with Prime Ministers, Heads of State and Royalty, as well as my chums, the trusty people who keep Number 10 and the Cabinet Office running smoothly. Let me take you through my cat-flap and show you a day in my very active political life...

Cat-Napping

The worst part of the day is the morning – I *hate* having to get out of my cosy bed. Especially after a busy night entertaining state dignitaries. Prime Ministers might be able to survive on hardly any sleep, but they've only got the one life to look after – I'm sleeping for nine! But it does help if I get my tummy rubbed. That's the purr-fect start to the day.

My day usually consists of keeping the machine of government well-oiled. Some observers seem to think the place runs on hot air! Truth is, I look after everyone – I think of myself as the *cat*alyst to making things happen. And with my background as a stray, I bring that common touch to the corridors of power which everyone agrees is so important.

I keep my own diary, just so people can't check up on me, and my engagements usually entail checking everyone is here who should be and eavesdropping on anything treacherous which might need reporting back to Him. Who needs a mole when you've got a cat on duty?

Fur flies over Humphrey's tale of

Humphrey the cat: A special fresh fish supper awaits the straying tom at Number 10

PETER OBORNE examines the defection of one of Mr Major's most trusted confidants

THE DEFECTION of Humphrey the Downing Street cat will go down as one of the great acts of political betrayal.

Ramsay Macdonald's reputation never recovered after he abandoned the Labour Party in the Thirties. The Gang of Four are still regarded as traitors for setting up the SDP in 1981. And Margaret Thatcher has never forgiven the Tory Cabinet which showed her the door of Downing Street in 1990.

But for sheer ingratitude, Humphrey's decision to leave the Downing Street home where he was loved and cherished for an army medical establishment is unmatched in modern political history.

For Humphrey was not simply loved, he was cherished by the staff of No 10. John Major even stood by the heartless creature during the

crisis of his long and distinguished Whitehall career when he faced a charge of cold-blooded murder of four robin chicks in the Downing Street garden. His thanks: an act of black-and-white hearted treachery. While Downing Street staff mourned his loss, the ungrateful animal was actually living a life of luxury in the Royal Army Medical College at Millbank.

There were conflicting views today about Humphrey's motives. One Whitehall source declared: "Not just the rats, even the cats are leaving the sinking ship." Some claimed he quit

Alive and

SERGEANT-M
Army Medical
Downing Str

mber of the Royal
Humphrey the
sks to the

EVENING STANDARD

TUESDAY, 26 SEPTEMBER, 1995   3

The   flap

tandard picture
e-unites Major
nd runaway pet

by NEIL TWEEDIE

despite the scandals, Humphrey remained a fixture in Downing Street.

Retired Major Marie Ellis said: "He was very bedraggled and at first we thought he didn't have an owner.

What's New, Pussycat?

I like to keep abreast of what's going on in the world.
We get all the papers. Usually those in charge are so busy,
other people here read the papers; they keep the
interesting bits – and show *them* the political coverage
instead. Truth is, politicians only get excited when *they*
are featured. Woe betide the backbencher who gets
more column inches than a Cabinet Minister!

In fact, even *I* get the cold shoulder when I make the
front page. I'm quite a celebrity these days. Of course,
you mustn't believe everything you read in the
newspapers – some of the things I have been accused
of simply are not true. Oh no, look – I've been doctored!
(Or rather, my photograph has.) Even pictures can lie
these days.

There are those who believe that if you put yourself up for
public office you must expect to be followed by the press.
Well *I* didn't put myself up for anything! I simply offered
my services as a mouser. And what happens? I can't even
go out for a night on the tiles now without being accused
of sleaze. Who are these sex kittens I'm supposed to hang
out with anyway? I wish...

The Cat's Eyes

This is my special vantage point, where I can keep my eye on who's coming and going. I know She wanted to have a balcony erected to enhance those photo opportunities, but you know what it's like getting planning permission to alter these listed buildings. Shame – I'd have liked somewhere to sit in the sun...

We do have to be careful at the windows though. With those long lenses you never know *what* you might get caught doing. It's no good getting him outside to tell some delegation from the RSPB that I'm not in if they can see me through the window.

You do need a pass these days even to enter the street – but the rabble still seem to get through. Still, I suppose they've got to hold their Cabinet meetings somewhere...

Choice Cuts

The Chancellor (Mr C. I call him) lives at Number 11 – very useful that, having your accountant next door. To be the Chancellor, you have to have a head for money (whatever that means – one with a slot in the top of it, presumably).

I often pop round when they forget to feed me. I can always rely on Mrs C. to give me something nice. She doesn't dare tell hubby though – he's on another economy drive, and if he knew she kept a few tins by... In fact, if he'd registered how many cats there are in the country and that most people keep them as a form of recreation, he'd probably have stuck duty on each tin by now.

Whenever I get the chance, I try to divert his attention from the catfood issue by whispering in his ear about reinstating the Dog Licence. He could use the revenue to buy himself a new briefcase for Budget Day. Still, like most of the bigwigs round here, he does have a very fashionable red lunchbox...and I really enjoy climbing into it whenever he leaves the lid open. It's really comfy for a quick nap in the middle of the day!

PROPERTY OF H.M. GOVERNMENT

Letting the Cat Out...

If I say so myself, I suppose you have to be fairly special to be Number 10's official mouser. But the red carpet's possibly going a bit far... The guy I feel sorry for is the one with the pointed hat on the door. He spends all day every day standing in front of the cameras yet is about as likely to get his picture in the Sunday papers as a minister without a mistress!

One of my main problems is getting in and out. This place is guarded like Fort Knox. (So if the US Bank's gold reserve goes missing, we'll know it's been taken by a reporter posing as a decorator...)

What would really make my life easier would be a catflap. I gather they did discuss it after the time I went walkabout, but there was argument about what colour it should be. Can't be red, blue, yellow or green – I'm supposed to be impartial. Catflaps don't come in black, and they feared grey might attract adverse comment!

Watch Out, Watch Out...

I do like to get a breath of fresh air occasionally.
Of course in London it's not as fresh as somewhere like
Huntingdonshire... A few months back I thought I might be
getting a trip out – there was talk about 'going to the country',
something about a Redwood, but that all fell through. Pity,
I was looking forward to a bit of tree climbing.

St James' Park is about as rural as it gets, and once
I've straightened my collar and checked my whiskers,
I'm ready to head off. I was accused of murdering a
duckling there a while back. Murder? Talk about over-
reaction! Anyway, serves it right for calling me a quack –
just because my honorary doctorate is still in the post...

The pleasing thing is that He stands up for me.
When some robins fell out of their nest in the Number 10
gardens, guess who was accused of birdlary?
'THE KILLER OF ST JAMES' STRIKES AGAIN',
they screamed. *He* was the only one to come to my
defence – He recognizes a cheep trick when he sees one!

The P.C. and the Mouse

One of my particular habits is finding somewhere warm
and dry to take a nap. In fact, you've probably seen
security men with those mirrors on long handles checking
that I'm not under any of the politicians' cars before they
drive off. My favourite place though has to be the
still-warm bonnet of a very large limousine!

In government, size is always so important. Ministers are impressed by either very large (cars, dinners, country houses, majorities) or very small (mobile phones, computers, unemployment figures, opposition parties). I've always reckoned small *is* beautiful – certainly in the world of espionage, the gadgets are getting smaller than ever.

In fact, they take it so seriously here that I've already been trained in the art of computer sabotage – I can identify and disable an enemy mouse in three seconds.

A Cautionary Tail

For a feeling of being at the hub of the real power base,
I occasionally manage to have a lie down on the Cabinet
table. The Cabinet Secretary gets very upset about it, as
he thinks I'll scratch it again. I keep telling him, 'M.T. woz
ere' was not carved by me!

The other reason they don't like me coming in here (apart
from the hairs) is in case I hear something I shouldn't.
I don't know who they think would be interested in what
they talk about. I can picture the headlines –
'CABINET SENSATION – MAJORITY WANT TEA
INSTEAD OF COFFEE'!

Did you know that once the Cabinet is in session, they lock
the doors and no one's allowed to leave, even to go to the
toilet? It all goes back to the time that one of them asked
the PM if he could pop out for a leak!

24

Keeping Up With the Windsors

They call the passageways of Downing Street the Corridors of Power. The only power that ever really surges down here at my level is when they're vacuuming. There's a whole army of housekeepers in Downing Street. You know, some of the Cabinet even complain about the cat hairs on the soft furnishings – yet they come in here with all manner of stains down their ties!

Anyway, I do take pride in my surroundings. I scratched a chunk out of the wallpaper and dug my claws in the skirting board in here just so they could justify to Mr C. next door getting the decorators in again. It's looking a treat now. They're going to do some trendy printing on the ceilings to finish it off. (It won't be the first time they've had spongers in here!)

In fact, it's looking so good they have discussed opening the place up to the public during the summer recess. Unfortunately Her Majesty got there first, and they reckon they wouldn't want to be seen jumping on any bandwagons. Funny, *I* thought that's what politics was all about...

The Cat's Whiskers

All the important personages who get to live in Number 10 usually end up with their painting on the wall. Their wives (or husband), who do a lot of the running around, are conspicuous by their absence when it comes to portraiture, and those of us with four legs, who actually run the place, normally fade into obscurity.

That is, until I came along. As the only member of the government (arguably any government) to have captured the hearts of a nation, I do believe I deserve to be immortalized on canvas.

People have different ideas about how to achieve immortality, of course. As I have, I'm sorry to say, had *the* operation (the Final Cut, as it's called), I cannot do it through my heirs – alas, we will never be a grandfather; taxidermy is *right* out of the question; and I would not give the pigeons the pleasure by allowing myself to be cast in bronze and erected in their flightpath.

Have I Got Mews For You?

Anything I tell the press has to be strictly on Lobby terms. They have to say 'Sources close to the Cabinet' or somesuch. Journalists love a good quote to support their stories. The trouble is, you can't always rely on them not to attribute *your* words to someone else.

Contrary to popular belief, it's not always the journalists' fault. In the past, a politician's quick '*No comment*' would suffice in shutting the press up. Now he or she will go all theatrical on you – show me an MP who *hasn't* come out with, 'You *might think that – I'm afraid I couldn't possibly comment.*' And then they wonder why they all get misquoted!

The trouble is, the press is not as discerning as it used to be – none of them know a good inside story when they hear it. Not so long ago I told a journalist of the scandal about the content of British catmeat – Brussels wanted to call it EUROCHUNKS. Talk about a threat to our sovereignty! And it never even made the tabloids...

Global Warming

The idea that I court publicity is preposterous. Did I ask for an obituary to be printed in *The Times* that time I went off to stay with friends in Millbank for three months? I simply thought that with our coming into line with the rest of Europe on everything, I'd take a three-month summer holiday like most of our continental cousins!

I do like to be photographed with famous people, though. Newspaper editors seem to think it's a game, however – they keep airbrushing me out of official photos! I'm still waiting for the call from *Hello* at the moment – I was approached by *The Cat* magazine, but it's not quite the same, is it? They had the cheek to tell me we all have to start somewhere!

I reckon if He really doesn't want me in the pictures, He should stand somewhere other than on my favourite step. You show me a cat who *doesn't* like sitting on the front doorstep in the sunshine and I'll show you a head of state who doesn't like standing in front of the cameras...

Having a Mice Day

I make a point of supervising the banqueting arrangements. When it comes to pampering people, one can only do it properly if one has first-hand experience of *being* pampered. And cats do know how to be pampered.

You also need to have breeding to take charge of these things. Which glass to use, which piece of cutlery to use first – did you know you work in to your dish from the outside? (Is this the solid stuff or the EPNS?) I try and get a say in the menu as well, just to make sure the leftovers are to my liking. I've persuaded chef to do duckling again tonight. Of course, when they've all gone there's nothing I like better than doing a spot of dribbling with a nice champagne cork. The shiny floors really help that game.

I also know my way round the wine cellar. I patrol it for big spiders and beetles. I'm supposed to catch mice, but I've never seen one. (Don't tell, or I'll be surplus to requirements.)

Chess Bored

You know, I'd love to be taken to the country retreat.
But because I belong to the Cabinet Office rather than the
PM, the nearest I get to Chequers is a chessboard. In fact,
they do say Chequers got its name from all the draughts
there, so I'm happy staying here at weekends. I have lots
of special people who all stay behind just to look after me.
At least, I let *them* think that!

Some believe the business of government is like a game
of chess, and those involved take it very seriously indeed.
However, I don't think anyone would dare say *'Check'*
or *'Mate'* to the Queen!

When I get the chance I try to influence important
decisions. When a Head of State comes to visit, my simply
making an appearance can alter the mood of the occasion –
Boris now asks after me by name, you know. Cats are
supposed to have a calming influence on people –
I wonder how many wars I've personally averted?

Curiosity...

Who said curiosity did a cat any harm? It always pays to keep abreast of what's going on in the world. Prime Minister's Question Time is a particular favourite of mine. *'I refer the honourable Member to the answer I gave a moment ago...'* Sterling stuff!

However, I do prefer radio over television – the advantage is you can be doing other things while listening to your favourite programmes. Most MPs prefer television being in the House as it gets them on the telly. Why else do you think they go into politics?

As for the cameras interfering with the business of government, you can tell from the strange background noises that nothing's changed over the years. *'Order! Order!'* There they go again – it's almost as rivetting as O.J.'s trial...

Weights and Pleasures

Being a celebrity, I find well-meaning people sometimes send me presents. It's very touching, though what they think I'm going to do with *another* tin of catfood I can't fathom. I quite enjoy an occasional catnip mouse however, though it is regarded as an illegal substance round here...

I have suffered from kidney problems, and my vet has put me on a strict diet. Trouble was, the diet sheet was in imperial measures – '6oz white fish' and so forth. The household had terrible trouble converting it for the shopping list now that retailers have had to go metric. They even summoned some fishmongers here (makes a change from rumour-mongers, I suppose).

It has been noted that on the whole I'm not a scrounger. No, I like to fend for myself. After the famous 'robin massacre' I have the feeling I'm being watched constantly these days – I'm sure they have a secret 'Eggs-File' on me. Or am I just being paranoid?

EURO
CHUNKS
METRIC
MOG
MUNCH

Socks' Appeal

The advantage of having me around is that I can offer advice on all manner of important subjects. When it comes to the tiniest bit of legislation, you wouldn't believe how many people get involved. I do my bit, vetting affairs of state on behalf of my peers. Where do you think the Dangerous Dogs Act came from?

Where I really come into my own is in the international arena. There is a network of communication between four-legged aides which is about as sophisticated as the InterNet. I have a 'special relationship' with my US counterpart Socks – although I'd rather not go into details. Suffice it to say, I'll be the first to know when he sits on the nuclear button!

I often hang around the fax machine – if it's about me, I like to read it first; if it's *for* me, I like to make sure no one else reads it! Trouble is, you can't always tell until we show it to the translator. Forget single currency, when are we going to push for a single language?

Affairs of State

Look at this lot. It's hard to tell whether they're serious news photographers or paparazzi. I know what they're like, all those pictures of me sitting pretty and they always select the one when I yawn, or lick my lips. Then they print it with a story saying I'm the aggressive bird-eating felon of old London town.

When I went AWOL and stayed with the Royal Army Medical Corps, it was the press who ended up getting me repatriated. It was only when they printed my picture in the paper that the military realized just who I was. They'd thought I was an old stray whose elderly owner 'must have died'!

Which just shows how well cut out for espionage this cat is. I might have been overdoing the bedraggled look, but I did get my way right inside the organization and won everyone's confidence. Like a true spy, I even slept with most of them! And to think that my cover was blown by a lousy picture in the paper...

44

Hair of the Cat

Inevitably, if you're in public life you do have to take a
pride in your appearance. Every time you walk past a
mirror you find yourself checking that your whiskers are
straight and your tail's not got anything caught up in it.
If there is a problem you have to attend to it
surreptitiously.

If you find a quiet corner you can give yourself a quick
once-over before re-entering the public gaze. Of course
no one takes any notice of the resident cat – I cannot count
the number of dignitaries I've seen adjusting themselves
prior to a meeting!

Some of course employ experts to style and coiffure
them – I do my own hair!

Reigning Cats and Dogs

I've never fathomed what Her Majesty sees in those dogs.
The corgi is the archetypal *canis horribilis*. Rather than a
dumb animal, Her Majesty should choose a cat as her pet.
We are fiercely loyal, though it's often discredited because
of our sharper sense of self-preservation. (I suppose that's
why cats like me are in politics...)

I have been wondering if there are any queens in the royal
household. (By which I mean female cats, of course.)
I wouldn't object to marrying into a rich family, and I'm
used to the public gaze. I'd probably get real cream with
my tea instead of that healthy vegetable substitute they
keep giving me.

Of course, I wouldn't begrudge an Honour if one's going.
I rather think *Sir* Humphrey sounds rather good. Still, it
always did. Why they forgot the 'Sir' when they
christened me I can't imagine...

The Big Sleep

At the end of a long day, I do enjoy a good 40 winks.
Most of my acquaintances go to the Lords to do this!
It's hard work being an influential political figure *and* a
role model. Talking of modelling, tomorrow I'm being
immortalised in resin for my doting public – no, not
Madame Tussauds, but *Humphrey in my Pocket*.
Another gruelling day ahead, by the sound of it...